GW00836097

Cheltenham College

French Idioms
and
Special Vocabulary

1900

This highly idiosyncratic French - English phrase book was first printed in 1897 and is here reprinted from a copy owned by Charles Grandorge Ewing (pupil at Cheltenham College May 1899-Easter 1901). The phrases for suggested use give a unique, often bizarre, but always highly amusing insight into the lives of young Edwardian gentlefolk.

Use of the College name is by kind permission of Mr John Richardson MA, Headmaster of Cheltenham College.

A short guide to Speaking and Writing French by Mr Taylor, Head of Modern Foreign Languages, Debenham High School, Suffolk, is included.

Published by Pasquapella Publications.

FRENCH

Iron, copper, tin and coal are found in England.

They returned from Peru last week.

We go to France and Portugal every year.

They are coming from Italy, they are in Paris.

My brother was born in India.

Prince Henry is on his way to Vienna, the capital of Austria.

The old Paris is not the Paris that you know.

London and Paris are the two most populous towns in Europe.

Lions and elephants live in Africa.

Nothing is more precious than health and patience.

A house without an orchard.

There they are without friends or money.

My father was a doctor.

He is an officer. They are fishermen.

IDIOMS

Le fer, le cuivre, l'étain et le charbon de terre se trouvent en Angleterre.

Ils sont revenus du Pérou la semaine dernière.

Nous allons tous les ans en France et au Portugal.

Ils viennent d'Italie, ils sont à Paris.

Mon frère est né aux Indes.

Le Prince Henri se rend à Vienne, capitale de l' Autriche.

Le vieux Paris n'est pas le Paris que vous connaissez.

Londres et Paris sont les deux villes les plus populeuses de l'Europe.

Les lions et les éléphants vivent en Afrique.

Rien n'est plus précieux que la santé et la patience.

Une maison sans verger.

Les voilà sans amis ni argent.

Mon père était médecin.

Il est officier. Ils sont pêcheurs.

He is an Italian. They are Belgians.

He has a thousand a year.

This cake is sold a franc a pound.

What a beautiful lawn! but there are no trees,

We have bought wine, beer, oil and prunes.

He has sold us good wine and excellent prunes.

Can you lend me some English novels?

She has fair hair and blue eyes.

The humming-bird with a red throat is very small.

His uncle, an old man of seventy-five, saved his life.

They had broken his arm. I had broken my left leg.

He has tooth-ache and a sore throat.

She has a head-ache that distresses her very much.

Yesterday was Sunday.

To-day is Easter Monday.

C'est un Italien. Ce sont des Belges.

Il a mille livres sterling par an.

Ce gâteau se vend un franc la livre.

Quelle belle pelouse! Mais il n'y a pas d'arbres.

Nous avons acheté du vin, de la bière, de l'huile et des pruneaux.

Il nous a vendu de bon vin et d'excellents pruneaux.

Pouvez-vous me prêter des romans anglais?

Elle a les cheveux blonds et les yeux bleus.

Le colibri à (la) gorge rouge est très petit.

Son oncle, vieillard de soixante-quinze ans, lui a sauvé la vie.

Ils lui avaient cassé le bras.

Je m'étais cassé la jambe gauche

Il a mal aux dents et à la gorge.

Elle a un mal de tête qui la fait beaucoup souffrir.

C'était hier dimanche.

C'est aujourd'hui le lundi de Pâques.

Who is that gentleman with the black whiskers? He is Mr. Poirier's son-in-law.

How many churches are there in this town?

There are ten, are there not?

Those children make too much noise.

Do not make so many mistakes.

The postman brings us many letters and little money.

Where does he live? At number eleven.

Our neighbour has as many horses as you.

They have given us much trouble.

Sunday, Monday, Tuesday, Wednesday, Thursday, Friday, Saturday.

January, February, March, April, May, June, July, August. September. October, November. December.

He does nothing for the greater part of the time.

Most men think little and speak a great deal.

Qui est ce monsieur aux favoris noirs? C'est le gendre de Monsieur Poirier.

Combien d'églises y a-t-il dans cette ville?

Il y en a dix, n'est-ce pas?

Ces enfants font trop de bruit.

Ne faites pas tant de fautes.

Le facteur nous apporte beaucoup de lettres et peu d'argent.

Où demeure-t-il? Au numéro onze.

Notre voisin a autant de chevaux que vous.

Ils nous ont donné bien de la peine.

Dimanche, lundi, mardi, mercredi, jeudi, vendredi, samedi.

Janvier, février. mars, avril, mai, juin, juillet, août, septembre, octobre, novembre décembre.

Il ne fait rien la plupart du temps.

La plupart des hommes pensent peu et parlent beaucoup.

All young people are imprudent.

All old people are suspicious.

That lady has an anxious look about her.
That lady appears to be anxious.
Those peaches look ripe.
Your sister sings out of tune. Not at all.
Our youngest soldiers and our best non-commissioned officers.
Our most seasoned soldiers and our boldest non-commissioned officers.
Those urchins are always going about bare-headed and barefooted.
Come at half-past two.
He has lost half a day.
They came at half-past twelve.
His late aunt was very distrustful.
I heard his late mother say that.
The last day of last year.

The Queen is very good to the poor.

Tous les jeunes gens sont imprudents.

Toutes les vieilles gens sont soupçonneux.

Cette dame a l'air inquiète.

Cette dame a l'air inquiète.

Ces pêches ont l'air mûres.

Votre soeur chante faux. Pas du tout.

Nos plus jeunes soldats et nos meilleurs sous-officiers.

Nos soldats les plus aguerris et nos sous-officiers les plus hardis.

Ces gamins vont toujours nu-tête et pieds nus.

Venez à deux heures et demie.
Il a perdu une demi-journée.

Ils sont arrivés a midi et demi.

Sa feue tante était très défiante.

J'ai entendu dire cela à feu sa mère.

Le dernier jour de l'année dernière.

La reine est très bonne pour les pauvres.

We are pleased with his success.

Why are you angry with his nephew?

Is she sorry for her conduct? I think so.

Are these plants good to eat?

We were very astonished at this news.

He will come on the first of June and will leave on the twenty-first of August.

Francis the first, Charles the fifth, and Henry the eighth were contemporaries.

The Russians had eighty men killed and five hundred wounded.

His daughter-in-law lives at number eighty.

That event happened in the year eighteen hundred.

He travelled more than two thousand miles on horseback.

Bring me a dozen eggs.

Will you have that egg fried or boiled?

They have lost thousands of sheep.

Nous sommes contents de son succès.

Pourquoi êtes vous fâché contre son neveu?

Est-elle fâchée de sa conduite? Je le crois.

Ces plantes sont elles bonnes à manger?

Nous avons été fort étonnés de cette nouvelle.

Il viendra le premier juin et partira le vingt et un août.

François premier, Charles quint et Henri huit étaient contemporains.

Les Russes eurent quatre-vingts hommes de tués et cinq cents de blessés.

Sa bru demeure au numéro quatre-vingt.

Cet événement eut lieu en l'an mille huit cent.

Il a fait plus de deux mille milles à cheval.

Apportez-moi une douzaine d'oeufs.

Voulez-vous cet oeuf sur le plat ou à la coque?

Ils ont perdu des milliers de brebis.

We shall start to-morrow
  fortnight.
He will arrive to-day week.
She died three months ago.
They have been here six weeks.
She has been abroad for six years.

I met them yesterday three
  weeks ago.
For more than forty days.
How long shall you stay here?

I read that book in an hour.
I shall call and see you in an
  hour's time.
How old is your grandfather?
He is not less than eighty-five
  years old.
He is older than my
  grandmother.
His horse works harder than
  three oxen.
A steeple a hundred feet high.

A steeple a hundred feet high.
A table two metres long.
That plank is two inches thick.

Nous partons de demain en quinze.

Il arrivera d'aujourd'hui en huit.

Elle est morte il y a trois mois.

Il y a six semaines qu'ils sont ici.

Elle est à l'étranger depuis six ans.

Je les ai rencontrés, il y a eu hier trois semaines.

Pendant plus de quarante jours.

Combien de temps resterez-vous ici?

J'ai lu ce livre en une heure.

Je passerai chez vous dans une heure.

Quel âge a votre grand-père?

Il n'a pas moins de quatre-vingt-cinq ans.

Il est plus âgé que ma grand' mère.

Son cheval travaille plus que trois boeufs.

Un clocher de cent pieds de haut (*or* de hauteur).

Un clocher haut de cent pieds.

Une table longue de deux mètres.

Cette planche a deux pouces d'épaisseur.

The pond is thirty feet deep.

Our drawing room is twenty feet long by fifteen wide.

That grocer is the richest man in the town.

Her elder brother is taller, stronger, and more active than my younger brother.

His eldest sister is a head taller than he.

His mother is as old as mine, but she is not so strong.

He has lost his youngest sister.

She has made fewer blunders than her brother.

His (*or* her) Majesty, and his (*or* her) Highness.

He has mislaid his grammar and mine.

She has found her dictionary and mine.

Your neighbours and ours.

Our enemies and yours.

My country and theirs.

They are richer than you think.

They are not less poor than you say.

L'étang a trente pieds de profondeur.

Notre salon a vingt pieds de long sur quinze de large.

Cet épicier est l'homme le plus riche de la ville.

Son frère aîné est plus grand, plus fort, et plus actif que mon frère cadet.

Sa soeur aînée a la tête de plus que lui.

Sa mère est aussi âgée que la mienne, mais elle n'est pas si forte.

Il a perdu sa soeur cadette.

Elle a fait moins de fautes que son frère.

Sa Majesté et son altesse.

Il a égaré sa grammaire et la mienne.

Elle a trouvé son dictionnaire et le mien.

Vos voisins et les nôtres.

Nos ennemis et les vôtres.

Ma patrie et la leur.

Ils sont plus riches que vous ne le croyez.

Ils ne sont pas moins pauvres que vous le dites.

Is he less conceited than he was?

The more the merrier.

The less rough the sea will be, the more pleasant it will be. I am so often sea-sick.

That Englishman is much taller than you are.

I shall go and see you as soon as possible.

I would sooner die than accept these terms.

She is not nearly such a miser as he is.

They will be none the happier for that.

I blame them all the more.

I alone am responsible.

I alone am responsible.

Will the butcher lend you his carriage?

He will not lend it to me to-morrow.

I consent he said, come and see me the day after tomorrow at latest.

Here are strawberries and cream. take some.

Do not take any there is not enough. Here is some.

Est-il moins vaniteux qu'il l'était?

Plus il y a de fous plus on rit.

Moins la mer sera houleuse, plus elle sera agréable. J'ai si souvent le mal de mer.

Cet Anglais est de beaucoup plus grand que vous.

J'irai vous voir le plus tôt possible.

Je mourrais plutôt que d' accepter ces conditions.

Elle n'est pas à beaucoup près aussi avare que lui.

Ils n'en seront pas plus heureux.

Je les en blâme davantage.

Je suis seul responsable.

Moi seul je suis responsable.

Le boucher vous prêtera-t-il sa voiture?

Il ne me la prêtera pas demain.

Je consens, dit-il, venez me voir après demain au plus tard.

Voici des fraises et de la crème, prenez-en.

N'en prenez pas, il n'y en a pas assez. En voici.

Give them back their pictures.
Do not give them back to them.

Give them back to them. There they are.
Do not send them to us.
Send them to us before the eleventh of July.
I have sent them to her; she has accepted them.
You stammer more than I do.
They are at home every Monday.
Neither he, nor she, nor I have seen the sea.
They did that against their will.
I who am unworthy of his friendship.
As for me, I do not believe it.
Who found this purse? They did.

It is not I, it is they.
Listen to him, place yourself there.
Do not listen to him, do not place yourself there.
Look at them. Do not look at them.
May you arrive in time!
They have directed me to you.
I am looking for a house.

Rendez-leur leurs tableaux. Ne les leur rendez pas.

Rendez-les-leur. Les voilà.

Ne nous les envoyez pas.
Envoyez-les-nous avant le onze juillet.
Je les lui ai envoyés ; elle les a acceptés.
Vous bégayez plus que moi.
Ils sont chez eux tous les lundis.
Ni lui, ni elle, ni moi nous n'avons vu la mer.
Ils ont fait cela malgré eux.
Moi qui suis indigne de son amitié.
Moi, je ne le crois pas.
Qui a trouvé cette bourse? Eux.
Ce n'est pas moi, ce sont eux.
Écoute-le, mets-toi là.

Ne l'écoute pas, ne te mets pas. là.

Regardez-les. Ne les regardez pas.
Puissiez-vous arriver à temps!
Ils m'on adressé à vous.
Je cherche une maison.

We applied to them.

Whose cottage is that ?-Hers.
Whose blackberries are these? - Nobodys.
A friend of theirs told them so the day before yesterday.
She has a bad leg.
Does his bad leg still pain him?
He raised his great arm and gave him a box in the ears.
Shut your eyes and hold out your hand.
Get up at once.
Do not get up before a quarter to twelve.
He says that, but he does not think it.
Which of these penknives do you prefer?
I like that one best.
I prefer the one you gave me.

Wait for them, they will be late.
Do not wait for them after halfpast twelve.
Read this. Pick up that.

Nous nous sommes adressés à eux.

À qui est cette chaumière? À elle.

À qui sont ces mûres? À personne.

Un de leurs amis le leur a dit avant hier.

Elle a mal à la jambe.

Sa jambe lui fait-elle toujours mal.

Il leva son grand bras et lui donna un soufflet.

Fermez les yeux et tendez la main.

Levez-vous tout de suite.

Ne vous levez pas avant midi moins un quart.

Il dit cela, mais il ne le pense pas.

Lequel de ces canifs préférez-vous?

J'aime mieux celui-là.

Je préfère celui que vous m'avez donné.

Attendez-les, ils seront en retard.

Ne les attendez pas après minuit et demi.

Lisez ceci. Ramassez cela.

Which of these landscapes do you like best, this, or that?

This watch cost more than your niece's.

What time was it? -It was half-past ten.

What sort of weather is it? It is very close.

At what time did she arrive?

At six o'clock in the morning by the express train.

On a fine summer night.-In the middle of winter.

What is the day of the month? Ask her.

What do you say? What do you see?

What prevents you from travelling?

The peasant of whom I have spoken to you.

The peasant to whose son I have written.

The barrister whose eloquence delighted them.

The barrister whose advice you are following.

Which way do you pass? This way or that way?

Lequel de ces paysages-aimez vous le mieux, celui-ci ou celui-là?

Cette montre a coûté plus cher que celle de votre nièce.

Quelle heure était-il? Il était dix-heures et demie.

Quel temps fait-il? Il fait très lourd.

À quelle heure est-elle arrivée?

À six heures du soir par le train express.

Par une belle nuit d'été. En plein hiver.

Le combien sommes-nous? Demandez-le-lui.

Qu'est-ce que vous dites? Que voyez-vous?

Qu'est-ce qui vous empêche de voyager?

Le paysan dont je vous ai parlé.

Le paysan au fils duquel j'ai écrit.

L'avocat dont l'éloquence les a charmés.

L'avocat dont vous suivez les conseils.

Par où passez-vous? Par ici ou par là?

What astonishes me is that he is still here.

What you say does not concern me.

That is what she complains of.

Of what does she complain, then? – What is the matter.

What are you thinking of? – What is the matter with you?

That is what I was thinking of.

Do what you are told.

What do you think of this idea?

What do you think of it?

Think over it at leisure.

Where do the swallows come from?

When do these birds go away? Where do they go?

Tell me what you think of it.

Think of it always never speak about it.

Whoever told you that lied.

Open any dictionary.

Take any two lines whatever.

The box in which I put away my letters.

The lady to whom we gave that present.

Ce qui m'étonne, c'est qu'il soit encore ici.

Ce que vous dites ne me regarde point.

C'est ce dont elle se plaint.

De quoi se plaint-elle donc? Qu'y a-t-il?

À quoi pensez-vous? Qu'avez-vous?

Voilà (ce) à quoi je songeais.

Faites ce qu'on vous dit.

Que pensez-vous de cette idée.

Qu'en pensez-vous?

Songez-y à loisir.

D'où viennent les hirondelles?

Quand ces oiseaux s'en vont-ils? Où vont ils?

Dites-moi ce que vous en pensez

Pensez-y toujours, n'en parlez jamais.

Quiconque vous a dit cela en a menti.

Ouvrez un dictionnaire quelconque.

Prenez deux lignes quelconques.

La boite dans laquelle (or où) je serre mes lettres.

La dame à qui (or à laquelle) nous avons fait ce cadeau.

What is that?–What is that music?

Don't ask me. It is the Germans perhaps.

Everything comes from America or Germany.

They were all killed.

Not one was saved.

The whole town is talking about it.

What a misfortune!–Nothing is more certain.

These workmen work all day.

These masons come every day.

They see each other every other day.

These persons were quite astonished and quite humbled.

They were quite surprised and quite ashamed.

I do not like ready made clothes.

She bought a ready made dress.

Nobody is pleased with his lot.

He has made no mistakes in his dictation.

Qu'est-cela? Quelle est cette musique?

Que sais-je! Ce sont peut-être les Allemands.

Tout nous vient de l'Amérique ou de l'Allemagne.

Ils ont tous été tués.

Pas un n'a été sauvé.

Toute la ville en parle.

Quel malheur! Rien n'est plus certain.

Ces ouvriers travaillent toute la journée.

Ces maçons viennent tous les jours.

Ils se voient tous les deux jours.

Ces personnes furent tout étonnées et tout humiliées.

Elles furent toutes surprises et toutes honteuses.

Je n'aime pas les habits tout faits.

Elle a acheté une robe toute faite.

Personne n'est content de son sort.

Il n'a pas fait de fautes dans sa dictée.

She has found a few mushrooms.

Here are a few.
Give me a little wine.
Give me a little.
These oranges cost a penny each.

Sufficient for the day is the evil thereof.
Everybody must please himself; everybody for himself.
Whatever discoveries he has made.
Whatever his discoveries may be.

However powerful these strangers are.
Some three hundred prisoners were taken.
The few animals which are found there are all ugly.
No one is perfect, and everyone complains.
Such an action; such words.
Such a fine action; such fine words.
I do not know any of them.

Neither of them has come.

Elle a trouvé quelques champignons.

En voici quelques-uns.

Donnez-moi un peu de vin.

Donnez-m'en un peu.

Ces oranges coûtent deux sous chacune.

À chaque jour suffit sa peine.

Chacun son goût; chacun pour soi.

Quelques découvertes qu'il ait faites.

Quelles que soient ses découvertes.

Quelque puissants que soient ces étrangers.

On a fait quelque trois cents prisonniers.

Les quelques animaux qu'on y rencontre sont tous laids.

Nul n'est parfait, et tout le monde se plaint.

Une telle action; de telles paroles

Une si belle action; de si belles paroles.

Je ne les connais ni les uns ni les autres.

Ni l'un ni l'autre ne sont arrivés.

Neither will be king.

These tradesmen have helped each other.

They have done each other much harm.

Hold your tongue, do not flatter yourself.

Something good; nothing better.

Whatever he may have done.

'What news? - I have seen nothing. - Nor I either.

Somebody ruined - nobody killed.

It will be so much saved.

Such a man as he is cannot consent to it.

You Turks are laughing at us.

A thing may be true and better left unsaid.

This office is to be let, that one is to be sold.

I have two lessons to give.

I have to translate two pages of Greek.

They have just received a hamper of game.

We had just been paying visits.

Ni l'un ni l'autre ne sera roi.

Ces marchands se sont aidés les uns les autres.

Ils se sont beaucoup nui les uns aux autres.

Taisez-vous, ne vous flattez pas.

Quelque chose de bon, rien de meilleur.

Quelque chose qu'il ait faite.

Quoi de nouveau? Je n'ai rien vu. - Ni moi non plus.

Quelqu'un de ruiné; personne de tué.

Ce sera autant d'épargné.

Un homme tel que lui ne saurait y consentir.

Vous autres turcs, vous vous moquez de nous.

Toute vérité n'est pas bonne à dire.

Ce bureau-ci est à louer, celui là est à vendre.

J'ai deux leçons à donner.

J'ai à traduire deux pages de Grec.

Ils viennent de recevoir une bourriche de gibier.

Nous venions de faire des visites.

I am very hungry and especially
very thirsty.

Are you not sleepy?

The doctor ought to come oftener.

He ought to have come sooner.

He might perhaps cure him.

One might perhaps have cured
him.

He must have started before
them.

He was to go to Africa.

He had to give up his enterprise.

We have been obliged to take
precautions.

They will get off with a fine.

How much do they owe him?

He will perhaps get off with two
months' imprisonment.

They went off arm in arm.

His studio is always topsyturvy.

It is the world upside down, in
my opinion.

Do what you will, you will not
succeed.

J'ai grand'faim et surtout grand'soif.

N'avez-vous pas sommeil?

Le médecin devrait venir plus souvent.

Il aurait dû venir plus tôt.

Il pourrait peut-être le guérir.

On aurait peut-être pu le guérir.

Il a dû partir avant eux.

Il devait aller en Afrique.

Il dut renoncer à son entreprise.

Nous avous dû prendre des précautions.

Ils en seront quittes pour une amende.

Combien lui doivent-ils?

Peut être en sera-t-il quitte pour deux mois de prison.

Ils partirent bras dessus bras dessous.

Son atelier est toujours sens dessus dessous.

C'est le monde renversé, à mon avis,

Vous aurez beau faire, vous ne réussirez pas.

He is not right, but you are wrong.

I fear he will be late.

Are you afraid we shall make a mistake?

We are not afraid you should make a mistake.

Do not be angry, I must go.

What is to be done! Where can one go! To whom can one apply!

He does not know what to do.

After swimming two leagues.

They oftener drive than walk.

You would learn faster if you attended to what you are told.

What questions was he asked.

I do not remember them.

Well! I remember them.

Do you? It is impossible.

If he comes, let me know.

If he had come, I should have sent them word.

I do not know whether he will return them to you.

Il n'a pas raison mais vous avez tort.

Je crains qu'il ne soit en retard.

Craignez-vous que nous nous trompions?

Nous ne craignons pas que vous vous trompiez.

Ne vous fâchez pas, il faut que je m'en aille.

Que faire? Où aller? À qui s'adresser?

II ne sait que faire.

Après avoir fait deux lieues à la nage.

Ils vont plus souvent en voiture qu'à pied.

Vous apprendriez plus vite, si vous faisiez attention à ce qu'on vous dit.

Quelles questions lui a-t-on faites?

Je ne me les rappelle pas.

Eh bien! je m'en souviens, moi.

Vraiment? C'est impossible.

S'il vient, faites-le moi savoir.

S'il était venu, je le leur aurais fait dire.

Je ne sais s'il vous les rendra.

When you come, I will tell you all about it.

He promised me he would write as soon as he arrived.

If your guardian should come, I would show him your exercises.

You are going to catch a cold, come in at once.

We shall do without vegetables.

He indulges in a little travelling now and then.

He took the wrong street, he ought to have turned to the right.

Is it my place to beg his pardon?

It is their turn to play.

He plays the violin, I play chess.

They are ever ready to abuse me.

She was very near accepting that place.

The ambassador is on the eve of his departure.

We were on the eve of moving.

She was studying whilst you were playing.

Quand vous viendrez, je vous
    raconterai l'affaire.
Il m'a promis qu'il écrirait
    aussitôt qu'il arriverait.
Si votre tuteur venait, je lui ferais
    voir vòs thèmes.

Vous allez vous enrhumer,
    rentrez tout de suite.
Nous nous passerons de légumes.
Il se passe un petit voyage de
    temps à autre.
Il s'est trompé de rue, il aurait dû
    prendre à droite.

Est-ce à moi de lui demander
    pardon?
C'est à eux à jouer.
Il joue du violon, je joue aux échecs.
Ils sont toujours prêts à
    m' injurier.
Elle a été bien près d'accepter
    cette place.
L'ambassadeur est à la veille de
    son départ.
Nous étions à la veille de
    déménager.
Elle était à étudier, tandis que
    vous étiez à jouer.

What do these young men, spend their time at?

They spend the time doing nothing.

On my arrival. On her departure.

In the open air. In the open sea.

In the very middle of the meadow.

I set about it in this manner.

Show me the manner in which he sets about it.

Be good enough to warn me in time.

We are not angry with them.

What a storm! They have had a narrow escape.

They were thought to be cured, but they gamble away worse - than ever.

In less than no time. In the twinkling of an eye.

Unawares. At a pinch. At random.

Stick no bills. No smoking allowed.

Always do your best.

Against the grain. Willy nilly.

Should it pour I would stay at home.

À quoi ces jeunes gens passent-ils
    leur temps?
Ils passent le temps à ne rien
    faire.
À mon arrivée. À son départ.
En plein air. En pleine mer.
Au beau milieu du pré.

Je m'y prends de cette manière.
Montrez-moi la façon dont il s'y
    prend.
Veuillez m'avertir à temps.

Nous ne leur en voulons pas.
Quel orage! Ils l'ont échappé
    belle.
On les croyait guéris, mais ils
    jouent de plus belle.

En moins de rien. En un clin
    d'oeil
À l'improviste. Au besoin. Au
    hasard.
Défense d'afficher. Défense de
    fumer.
Faites toujours de votre mieux.
À contre coeur. Bon gré mal gré.
S'il pleuvait à verse, je resterais à
    la maison.

Come and see me every Sunday.

Rest a little before starting off again.
You like reading, do you not?
He is not at home in the evening, is he?
She is French by birth.-Is she?

The general's grandfather on his mother's side was a miller by trade.
We were about to sail for Spain.

You must give him back his gun.

What do they want to be less unhappy?
They want a little more patience.
For that, we should require a better crew.
He lacks courage and wants money.
You will succeed by working nine hours a day.
He thinks too much of himself, he will fail.
He began by flattering them, he ended by insulting them.

ʳ tous les dimanches.

ıs un peu avant de

z la lecture, n'est-ce pas?
ıs chez lui le soir, n'est-
s?

L ̣ st française de naissance. -
Vraiment?

L'aïeul maternel du général était
meunier de son état.

Nous allions faire voile pour
l'espagne.

Il faut que vous lui rendiez son
fusil.

Que leur faut-il pour être moins
malheureux?

Il leur faut un peu plus de patience.

Pour cela, il nous faudrait un
meilleur équipage.

Il manque de courage, et il a
besoin d'argent.

Vous réussirez en travaillant neuf
heures par jour.

Il s'en fait accroire, il échouera.

Il commença par les flatter, il finit
par les insulter.

Was the redoubt within cannon
range?
It was half way up the hill, out of
range.
Water began to fail them.

Will this shepherd be in a
position to earn his living? We
hope so.
He will manage to obey them.
I was groping my way along.
Do not walk backwards.
You will fall backwards.
But for them but for their
generous help we were lost.
He is rather a coward.
He never remembers that date.

I do not like his face.
I do not recollect his name.
He never remembers that date.
The captain was nearly drowned.
He was nearly drowned.
He is far from rich.

He is not cured, far from it.
The enemy had blown up the
bridge.

La redoute était-elle à portée de canon?

Elle était à mi-côte, hors de portée.

L'eau commençait à leur manquer.

Ce berger sera-t-il à meme de gagner sa vie? Nous l'espérons.

Il fera en sorte de leur obéir.

Je m'avançais à tâtons.

Ne marchez pas à reculons.

Vous tomberez à la renverse.

Sans eux, sans leur généreux secours nous étions perdus.

Il est tant soit peu lâche.

Il ne se souvient jamais de cette date.

Sa figure ne me revient pas.

Son nom ne me revient pas.

Il ne se rappelle jamais cette date.

Le capitaine faillit se noyer.

Peu s'en fallut qu'il ne se noyât.

Il s'en faut de beaucoup qu'il soit riche.

Il n'est pas guéri, tant s'en faut.

L'ennemi avait fait sauter le pont.

Where was the powder mag-
azine which they blew up.
How dare you assert that.
You should have faced all perils.

Have they enjoyed themselves?
We rejoice at your success.

Your success rejoices us.
They enjoy every privilege.
We shall give him a ridingwhip
on his name-day.
That forest stretches out of sight.
The robbers rushed sword in
hand.
Better late than never.
I think it is a most strange event.

He did not do it on purpose. Yes
he did.
Is he not mistaken ?-It is possible.

Do not do it again.
I shall not see him again.
It is possible we are mistaken.

It may be. One must make sure of
nothing.

Où était la poudrière qu'ils ont fait sauter?

Comment osez-vous soutenir cela?

Vous auriez dû braver tous les périls.

Se sont-ils bien amusés?

Nous nous réjouissons de votre succès.

Votre succès nous réjouit.

Ils jouissent de tous les privilèges.

Nous lui ferons cadeau d'une cravache pour sa fête.

Cette forêt s'étend à perte de vue.

Les voleurs s'élancèrent l'épée à la main.

Mieux vaut tard que jamais.

Je pense que c'est un événement des plus étranges.

Il ne l'a pas fait exprès. Si.

Ne se trompe-t-il pas? C'est possible.

Ne le faites plus.

Je ne le reverrai plus.

Il est possible que nous nous trompions.

Cela se peut. Il ne faut jurer de rien.

48

Those natives live on game and
fish.
That artist lives from hand to
mouth.
Napoleon was at the height of his
power.
What is the good of cursing fate?
What is the use of getting out of
patience?
She is getting deafer and deafer.

They burst into tears.
I burst out laughing.
I knew them to be proud and
obstinate.
It is all the worse on his part.
I shall turn that circumstance to
good account.
Then indeed, it is a set purpose.
You will have to be resigned to it.

The City of London sided with
the Parliament.
He takes after his grandmother.
Do you value this violin very
much?
I do not value it in the least.

Ces indigènes vivent de gibier et
de poisson.

Cet artiste vit au jour le jour.

Napoléon était au comble de sa
puissance.

À quoi bon maudire le sort?

À quoi sert de s'impatienter?

Elle devient de plus en plus .
sourde.

Elles fondirent en larmes.

J'éclatai de rire.

Je les savais fiers et entêtés.

C'est d'autant plus mal de sa part

Je tirerai un bon parti de cette
circonstance.

Décidément c'est un parti pris.

Il faudra bien en prendre votre
parti.

La ville de Londres prit parti
pour le parlement.

Il tient de sa grand'mère.

Tenez-vous beaucoup à ce
violon?

Je, n'y tiens pas le moins du monde.

It is best to say nothing about it.

The troops took possession of the citadel.

After fighting indifferently they begged for mercy.

After resting they set out again.

They have quarrelled; they are even daggers drawn.

It is then war to the knife.

The savages were armed with bows and lances.

You will learn French in course of time.

The more you will complain, the less people will pity you.

Come early.

That's right! There you are sensible.

He is always good-tempered.

The Crusaders set out in the Spring.

Do not go there in Summer.

These shopkeepers vie with one another in swindling.

Answer them by return of post.

Il vaut mieux n'en rien dire.

Les troupes se sont emparées de la citadelle.

Après avoir combattu tant bien que mal, ils demandèrent grâce.

Après s'être reposés, ils se remirent en route.

Ils sont brouillés, ils sont même à couteaux tirés.

C'est donc la guerre à outrance.

Les sauvages étaient armés d'arcs et de lances.

Vous apprendrez le français avec le temps.

Plus vous vous plaindrez moins on aura pitié de vous.

Venez de bonne heure.

À la bonne heure! Vous voilà raisonnable !

Il est toujours de bonne humeur.

Les croisés partirent au printemps.

N'y allez pas en été.

Ces boutiquiers volent à qui mieux mieux.

Repondez-leur courrier par courrier.

Acknowledge the receipt of this letter by return of post.

They starved their victims to death.

Send for the surgeon.

I have a sprain, but it will be nothing.

It is late. It is getting late.

It is daylight. It is dark.

The sun is shining. The moon is shining.

It is hotter than in Australia.

These children are too dainty.

Winter is over. The nations are at war.

I wish you to stay till tomorrow.

That is no business of yours.

Mind your business.

There are three wheels broken. So much the worse.

They have hurt themselves.

It serves them right.

How wicked you are!

They seem to be comfortably off.

Do not be too sure of it.

Accusez-moi réception de cette
lettre par le retour du courrier.
Ils firent mourir leurs victimes de
faim.
Faites venir le chirurgien.
J'ai une entorse, mais cela ne sera
rien.
Il est tard. Il se fait tard.
Il fait jour. Il fait nuit.
Il fait soleil. Il fait clair de lune.

Il fait plus chaud qu'es Australie.
Ces enfants sont trop difficiles.
L'hiver est fini. Les nations sont
en guerre.
Je désire que vous restiez jusqu'
à demain.
Cela ne vous regarde pas
Mêlez-vous de vos affaires.
Il y a trois roues de cassées. Tant
pis.
Ils se sont fait mal.
C'est bien fait.
Que vous êtes méchant!
Ils ont l'air d'être à leur aise.
Ne vous y fiez pas.

He is very free and easy. he
  always makes himself at home.
What is the matter with him.
  then?-He is in a rage.
What is the matter?-I do not
  know at all. Post this letter.
Go and see, some misfortune has
  happened.
Whose is that? It is mine.
I never wait for my friends.
I always wait for them.
I expect him to be ploughed.

He has not passed; I expected it.
Has he enough to pay his debts?
I very much doubt it.
I doubt his honesty.
I apologize.
Don't mention it.
There were no railways eighty
  years ago.
More than two hundred years
  elapsed.
Do not shrug your shoulders in
  that manner.
Set your clock by my watch.

It is a few minutes fast.

Il est bien sans gêne, il fait
toujours comme chez lui.
Qu' a-t-il donc? Il est en colère

Qu'y a-t-il? Je n'en sais rien.
Mettez cette lettre à la poste.
Allez voir. Il est arrivé quelque
malheur.
A qui est cela? C'est à moi.
Je n'attends jamais mes amis.
Moi, je les attends toujours.
Je m'attends à ce qu'il fasse fruit
sec.
Il a été refusé; je m'y attendais.
A-t-il de quoi payer ses dettes?
J'en doute fort.
Je doute de son honnêteté.
Je vous fais mes excuses.
Il n'y a pas de quoi.
Il n'y avait pas de chemins de fer,
il y a quatre-vingts ans.
Il se passa plus de deux cents ans.

Ne haussez pas les épaules de
cette manière.
Réglez votre pendule sur ma
montre.
Elle avance de quelques minutes.

Mine is half-an-hour slow.

They were running with all their might.

As for me, I was shouting at the top of my voice.

At whose house does your . friend live?

He was born on the twenty first of August eighteen hundred.

Give the dog some water, the heat makes it thirsty.

I shall go the day after tomorrow to bid them goodbye.

Ring, knock, he is hard of hearing.

I have been told more than once that he bears me a grudge.

Let the worst come to the worst. In the middle of the marsh.

Better and better. Worse and worse. From day to day.

From time to time. In plenty.

These farmers are much to be pitied.

I rented his house just as it was.

La mienne retarde d'une demi-
heure.

Ils couraient de toutes leurs
forces.

Quaint à moi, je criais à tuetête.

Chez qui demeure votre ami?

Il est né le vingt et un août mille
huit cent.

Donnez de l'eau au chien, la
chaleur l'altère.

J'ïrai après demain leur faire mes
adieux.

Sonnez, frappez, il a l'oreille
dure.

On m'a dit plus d'une fois qu'il
m'en veut.

Au pis aller. Au milieu du marais.

De mieux en mieux. De pis en pis.
De jour en jour.

De temps en temps. À foison.

Ces métayers sont bien à
plaindre.

J'ai loué sa maison telle quelle.

That waiter gets many tips.

Post this letter before twelve o'clock.

He married the daughter of our chimney sweep.

When is your cousin going to get married?

I don't care. Three times out of five.

He likes riding.

I prefer driving.

How much does this beautiful fruit sell for.

Ask her.

One says that every day.

One does not do that sort of thing. How is it that he is here?

Let us take the eleven-forty train.

I did so to please them.

She does not like that gentleman, does she?

The orderly passed by at full gallop.

Whom are you angry with?

In spite of our losses and misfortunes.

Ce garçon reçoit beaucoup de pourboires.

Mettez cette lettre à la poste avant midi.

Il a épousé la fille de notre ramoneur.

Quand votre cousine va-t-elle se marier?

Cela m'est égal. Trois fois sur cinq.

I1 aime à monter à cheval.

J'aime mieux me promener en voiture.

Combien se vendent ces beaux fruits?

Demandez-le-lui.

Cela se dit tous les jours.

Cela ne se fait pas. Comment se fait iI qu'il soit ici?

Prenons le train de onze heures quarante.

Je l'ai fait pour leur faire plaisir.

Ce monsieur ne lui plait pas, n'est-ce pas?

L'ordonnance passa ventre-à-terre.

À qui en avez-vous?

Malgré nos pertes et nos malheurs.

Along the canal. Three times in succession.

By dint of pluck and foresight.

For want of cavalry. As a makeshift.

At the public expense.

With respect to her son-in-law.

At my expense. With respect. to him.

In the public service. By day and by night.

The capital was taken by storm.

The garrison was put to the sword.

She took it into her head to become a nun.

He was coming up four steps at a time. Step by step.

He was going on all fours. Dry-shod.

Is the mare rough-shod?

Between us three we shall manage it.

The prisoners filed off in pairs.

God forbid! Reluctantly.

Le long du canal. Trois fois de
  suite.

À force de courage et de
  prévoyance.

Faute de cavalerie. Faute de
  mieux.

Aux frais de l'état.

À l'égard de son gendre.

À mes frais. À son égard.

Au service de l'état. De jour et de
  nuit.

La capitale fut prise d'assaut.

La garnison fut passée au fil de
  l'epée.

Elle se mit en tête de se faire
  religieuse.

Il montait quatre a quatre. Pas à
  pas.

Il allait à quatre pattes. À pied
  sec.

La jument est-elle ferrée à glace.

À nous trois nous en viendrons à
  bout.

Les prisonniers défilèrent deux à
  deux.

À Dieu ne plaise! À mon corps
  défendant.

By your leave. By ten o'clock.

Were I to see him begging!

The pedestrians were running away as fast as their legs would carry them.

I have killed two birds with one stone.

A hand to hand fight followed.

These reapers work and rest by turns.

The farmer was ploughing.

Such a trade soon wears out a man.

What history do you use?

You should have got into shelter.

You would have had to go to expense.

He who thinks only of himself has no friends.

I would not take that horse as a gift.

The regiment had not yet been in action.

The battle was fought on the first of April.

Ne vous en déplaise! À dix heures.

Dussé-je le voir mendier !

Les piétons se sauvaient à toutes
jambes.

J'ai fait d'une pierre deux coups.

Il s'ensuivit un combat corps à
corps.

Ces moissonneurs travaillent et
se reposent tour à tour.

Le fermier était en train de
labourer.

Un tel métier (vous) use vite un
homme.

De quelle histoire vous servez
vous ?

Il fallait vous mettre à l'abri.

Il vous aurait fallu faire des
dépenses.

Qui ne pense qu'à soi n'a pas
d'amis.

Je ne voudrais pas de ce cheval.
quand on me le donnerait.

Le régiment n 'avait pas encore
donné.

La bataille fut livrée le premier
avril.

In the open field. To place in the field.

Our field-artillery. To take the field.

Come again in a week's time at latest.

They were assailed on all sides.

Many men were lost on either side.

Tell them that from me.

It is the lion's share.

He is extremely selfish.

We shall go for an excursion next week, will you join us?

What a pity you live so far away!

He gives himself the airs of a rich man, but he has great difficulty in making both ends meet.

The Conservative party have been in power for several Years.

I am anxious to show you my greenhouses.

You will have to find other means.

En rase campagne. Mettre en campagne.

Notre artillerie de campagne. Se mettre en campagne.

Revenez dans une huitaine au plus tard.

Ils furent assaillis de toutes parts.

On perdit bien du monde de part et d'autre.

Dites-leur cela de ma part.

C'est la part du lion.

Il est on ne peut plus égoïste.

Nous ferons une partie de plaisir la semaine prochaine, voulez vous en être?

Quel dommage que vous demeuriez si loin!

Il fait le riche, mais il a beaucoup de peine a joindre les deux bouts.

Le parti conservateur est au pouvoir depuis plusieurs années.

Je tiens à vous montrer mes serres.

Il faudra que vous trouviez d'autres moyens.

That does not matter. They vie with one another in working.

What have you done with your guns?

What has he done with them?

How far is it from here to Bristol?

It is quite ten leagues

Is it long since that accident happened?

Never go out on an empty stomach.

He has invested his money at five per cent. In an annuity.

These light blue stuffs are cheap.

How much did you pay for those straw-coloured gloves?

The Emperor and the court had a bad reception.

Why were they not given a good reception?

When will these gentlemen be back?

On the day before they were in Rome, on the third day in Corsica.

Speech is silver, but silence is gold.

Cela ne fait rien, ils travaillent à l'envi.

Qu'avez-vous fait de vos fusils?

Qu 'en a-t-il fait?

Combien y a-t-il d'ici a Bristol?

Il y a bien dix lieues.

Y a-t-il longtemps que cet accident est arrivé?

Ne sortez jamais à jeun.

Il a placé son argent à cinq pour cent. En rente viagère.

Ces étoffes bleu clair sont bon marché.

Combien avez-vous payé ces gants paille?

L'empereur et la cour furent mal reçus.

Pourquoi ne leur a-t-on pas fait bon accueil.

Quand ces messieurs seront-ils de retour?

La veille ils étaient à Rome, le surlendemain en Corse.

La parole est d'argent, mais le silence est d'or,

Does he sometimes let you hear
from him?

Once a year at most.

We have not seen him for five and
a half years.

He longs to see them again.

Everything comes to him that
waits.

If you will take my word. you
will not go.

Did the carriage suit you?

Did you agree about the price?

Give them that into the bargain.

They got off cheap.

It is freezing hard enough to to
break stones.

Thanks to them we shall lose
nothing.

He does good and evil without
thinking.

That drink has made them ill.

They made themselves masters of
the town.

Do you know them by sight?

I am always thinking of those
poor sailors.

So am I. How much they are to be
pitied!

Vous donne-t-il quelquefois de ses nouvelles?

Une fois par an tout au plus.

Il y a cinq ans et demi que nous ne l'avons vu.

Il lui tarde de les revoir.

Tout vient à celui qui sait attendre.

Si vous m'en croyez, vous n' irez pas.

La voiture vous a-t-elle convenu?

Êtes-vous convenus du prix?

Donnez-leur cela pardessus le marché.

Ils en ont été quittes à bon marché.

Il gèle à pierre fendre.

Grâce à eux nous ne perdrons rien.

Il fait le bien et le mal sans réfléchir.

Cette boisson les a rendus malades.

Ils se rendirent maîtres de la ville.

Les connaissez-vous de vue?

Je pense toujours à ces pauvres marins.

Moi aussi. Qu'ils sont à plaindre!

He began to weep bitterly.

Tell him he will have to deal with
me.
He does not answer for success.
Nor I either. He does not know
what he is talking about.
What is the matter?
It concerns his happiness. His life
is at stake.
The thing was to fight.
I cannot help admiring them.

I cannot help it.
I cannot help it; everything is
going without let or hindrance.
What can I do? What do I know?
I am tired out. Do you feel sick?

Your friend requires much
pressing.
He had designs upon my purse.
Where there's a will there's a way.
We will take them there with
pleasure.
Living on fruits and vegetables,
they spend little.

Il se mit à pleurer à chaudes larmes.

Dites-lui qu'il aura affaire à moi.

Il ne répond pas du succcès.

Ni moi non plus. Il parle à tort et à travers.

De quoi s'agit-il?

Il s'agit de son bonheur. Il y va de sa vie.

Il s'agissait de combattre.

Je ne puis m'empêcher de les admirer.

Je ne puis m'en empêcher.

Je n'y puis rien ; tout va à vau l'eau.

Qu'y puis-je? Que sais-je?

Je n'en peux plus. Avez-vous mal au coeur?

Votre ami se fait bien prier.

Il en voulait à ma bourse.

Vouloir c'est pouvoir.

Nous les y conduirons avec plaisir.

Vivant de fruits et de légumes, ils dépensent peu.

He found them still alive.

He was skating, he is wonderfully well.

I am very fond of bathing in the sea.

We persevere in the hope of succeeding.

Fishing and shooting will do him good.

He is fond of fishing, I prefer shooting.

What New Year's present have you chosen?

We have chosen Sir Walter Scott's novels.

Two of our friends have been elected.

These girls liked each other as soon as they saw each other.

The sentry let us pass.

The wretch would have allowed us to be killed.

They allowed themselves to be shot by hundreds.

They let themselves slip down to the ground.

Three kings of the same name had succeeded each other.

That poetry is very beautiful, I have heard it read.

Il les a trouvés encore vivants.

Il était à patiner, il se porte à merveille.

J'aime beaucoup à me baigner dans la mer.

Nous persévérons dans l'espoir de réussir.

La pêche et la chasse lui feront du bien.

Il aime la pêche, moi je préfère la chasse.

Quelles étrennes avez-vous choisies.

Nous avons choisi les romans de Sir Walter Scott.

Deux de nos amis ont été élus.

Ces jeunes filles se sont plu, aussitôt qu'elles se sont vues.

La sentinelle nous a laissés passer.

Le misérable nous aurait laissé tuer.

Ils se sont laissé fusiller par centaines.

Ils se sont laissés glisser jusqu' à terre.

Trois rois du même nom s'étaient succédé.

Cette poésie est très belle, je l'ai entendu lire.

That lady reads very well, I have heard her read.

I am sorry for the trouble he has given himself.

We have made them travel.

We have made them learn physics.

I have had a wheelbarrow made.

She had a dress made.

Get Henry to do that.

The duke had taken them prisoners.

What a shower. I am soaking wet and covered with mud.

The English fought with dogged obstinacy.

There was no ford at that place.

We left off from sheer weariness.

He took heart of grace.

The look-out man was fast asleep.

Leave him alone, he is an acquaintance of mine.

It is said they have become bankrupt. What has become of them?

Cette dame lit très bien, je l'ai entendue lire.

Je regrette la peine qu 'il s'est donnée.

Nous les avons fait voyager.

Nous leur avons fait apprendre la physique.

J'ai fait faire une brouette.

Elle s'est fait faire une robe.

Faites faire cela à Henri.

Le duc les avait faits prisonniers.

Quelle averse! Je suis trempé jusqu'aux os et convert de boue.

Les Anglais se battirent avec acharnement.

Il n'y avait pas de gué à cet endroit.

Nous nous arrêtâmes de guerre lasse.

Il fit contre mauvaise fortune bon coeur.

La vigie dormait à poings fermés.

Laissez-le tranquille, c'est une de mes connaissances.

On dit qu'ils ont fait banqueronte. Que sont ils devenus?

I have heard of their bankruptcy.
I have heard that he was head
and ears in debt.
I have been told so, but I do not
believe a word of it.
The fire is out, light the gas.
Set a thief to catch a thief,
It is six of the one and half a
dozen of the other.
Say what you will, you will not
manage it.
He is like his cousin. They are as
like as two peas.

Birds of a feather flock together.
He is very witty, but he is
constantly slandering his
neighbour (his fellow man).
What of that?
My feet are frozen, and I am
famished.
He is a chip of the old block, he
smokes from morning till night.

J'ai entendu parler de leur faillite.

J'ai entendu dire qu'il était criblé
de dettes.

On me l'a dit, mais je n'en crois
rien.

Le feu est éteint, allumez le gaz.

A voleur voleur et demi.

C'est bonnet blanc blanc bonnet.

Vous avez beau dire, vous n'en
viendrez pas à bout.

Il ressemble à son cousin. Ils se
ressemblent comme deux
gouttes d'eau.

Qui se ressemble s'assemble.

Il a beaucoup d'esprit, mais il
médit sans cesse du prochain.
Que voulez-vous?

J'ai les pieds gelés, et je meurs de
faim.

Il chasse de race, il fume du matin
au soir.

VOCABULARY.

SUBSTANTIVES.

la filasse	tow
le rejeton	shoot, offspring
l'enjouement, m.	playfulness
l'engouement, m.	infatuation
le trainard	straggler
l'engrenage, m.	gear
le naufrage	shipwreck.
le réseau	network, system
l'atelier, m.	workshop, studio team,
l'attelage, m.	yoke
l'avarie, f.	damage
la cravache	horse-whip
le cercueil	coffin
la fondrière	quagmire
la fonderie	foundry
le grabat	pallet
le débarras	riddance [water
la nappe	table-cloth, sheet of
l'ornière, f.	rut, track
le cerf	stag
le cerveau	brain, head
la cervelle	brains
le crâne	skull, swaggerer
le potage	soup [stove
le potager	kitchen-garden, kitchen
le frimas	hoar frost
le joug	yoke [crew
l'équipage, m.	equipage, carriage,
le métayer	petty farmer
l'abonnement, m.	subscription
le verglas	glazed frost
le verger	orchard
la chute	fall
la rechute	relapse
la fantassin	foot-soldier
l'arçon, m.	saddle bow
l'étrier, m.	stirrup
l'éperon, m.	spur
le créneau	battlement
la meurtriére	loop-hole
l'etau, m.	vice

l'etal, m.	butcher's stall, shop
l'hélice, f.	screw
la vis	screw
l'étage, m	story, floor
l'étagère, f.	set of shelves
l'éclaircie, f.	glade, clear spot
La clairière	glade
l'éclaireur, m.	scout
l'escarmouche, f.	skirmish
l'échauflourée	affray
la lisière	border, skirt
l'étang, m.	pond
le corbillard	hearse, young raven
le coupe-gorge	cut-throat place, den of thieves
le cabotier	coaster (ship)
le caboteur	coaster (sailor)
le cabotin	strolling player
la tignasse	old wig
la lie	lees, dregs
le chambranie	door-case, window-frame, chimney piece
le bouvier	ox-driver
la fanal	ship's lantern, beacon
le falot	large lantern
le phare	light-house, beacon
la nageoire	fin
l'écluse, f.	mill dam, lock, sluice
le cirage	waxing, blacking
le sillon	furrow, wake
le sillage	head-way, wake
le trépas	death
le seigle	rye
l'avoine, f.	oats
le blé	corn, wheat
le froment	wheat
l'orge, f.	barley
le pain bis	brown bread
la paille	straw, flaw
le foin	hay
le fléau	flail, scourge
le pourpoint	doublet
la boutique	shop
le magasin	shop, warehouse, magazine
l'haleine, f.	breath
le remorqueur	tow-boat
la rancune	spite, rancour
le taudis	hovel, dog-hole

la masure	ruins, hovel l
la cicatrice	scar
la balafre	gash, scar
la mansarde	garret
le galetas	garret, hole.
la vague	wave
l'écueil, m.	rock, danger
la falaise	cliff
le réçif	reef
la berge	steep bank
la lame	blade, plate, wave
la trombe	water-spout
le tourbillon	whirlwind, whirlpool
le remous	eddy
le repaire	den, lair, haunt
le gîte	home, lodging, form
la dalle	flag-stone
la cave	cellar
le tertre	rising ground, hillock
le talus	slope
l'antre, m.	cave
la buanderie	wash-house
le linge	linen
le pansement	dressing, grooming
le vacarme	hubbub
le métier	trade, frame, loom
le charron	wheel-wright
le menuisier	joiner
le charcutier	pork-butcher
le boucher	butcher
le boulanger	baker
l'épicier, m.	grocer
l'ébéniste, m.	cabinet-maker
le vitrier	glazier
le verrier	glass-founder
le charpentier	carpenter
le forgeron	blacksmith
le teinturier	dyer
le quincaillier	iron-monger
le tisserand	weaver
le maréchal (ferrant)	farrier
le brasseur	brewer
le ferblantier	tinman
le cordonnier	shoemaker
le savetier	cobbler
l'orfèvre, m.	goldsmith
le serrurier	locksmith
le meunier	miller

le bûcheron	wood-cutter
le bateleur	juggler, buffoon
le batelier	boatman
l'équarrisseur, m.	knacker
la bûche	log, blockhead (stake
le bûcher	wood shed, funeral pile,
le commensal	guest, boarder
le chiffonnier	ragman
la râpe	rasp
le rabat	plane
la lime	file
la scie	saw
le marteau	hammer
le ciseau	chisel, scissors
la vrille	gimlet
le vilebrequin	wimble
le billot	block
la faux	scythe
le copeau	chip
l'entorse, f.	sprain
le légume	vegetable (wardens
la jurande	wardenship, body of
la maîtrise	freedom of a trade
la caserne	barracks
la lucarne	dormer window
le guichet	wicket
le gué	ford
l'autel, m.	altar
la charpie	lint
la ouate	wadding, padding
le tournai	tournament
le chardon	thistle
l'ortie, f.	nettle
la ronce	bramble
les broussailles, f.	brush-wood
la bruyère	heath
la fougère	fern
le lierre	ivy
le roseau	reed
le jonc	rush
l'ajonc, m.	furze
le champignon	mushroom
le nénuphar	waterlily
l'usine, f.	manufactory, works
l'entrave, f.	trammel, obstacle
le cuivre, f.	copper, brass
le cuir	leather, strop
l'acier, m.	steel

l'etain, m.	tin, pewter
le bourgeon	bud, pimple [wood
l'amadou, m.	German tinder, touch
la massue	club
le gourdin	cudgel
la boue	mud
la fange	mire
le colporteur	hawker, pedlar
le butin	booty
l'anse, f.	handle, creek
la nef	nave
le linceul	shround
la transe	fright
la giberue	cartridge-box
le ceinturon	sword-belt
le baudrier	shoulder-belt
le bégayement	stammering
la surdité	deafness
la cécité	blindness
la calvitie	baldness
l'inimitié, f.	enmity [net
l'épervier, m.	sparrow-hawk, sweep
le filet	thread, net
le fil d'archal	iron-wire
l'archet, m.	bow (violin)
le bourreau	executioner
la cuisse	thigh
l'aine, f.	groin
la pierrement. d' achoppement	stumbling-block
la mousse	moss froth
le mousse	cabin-boy
la pelouse	lawn
le gazon	turf
le milan	kite (bird)
le cerf-volant	kite (toy)
le brevet	patent
le vautour	vulture [theatre
le parterre	flower-garden, pit of a
le ramier	wood-pigeon
le rameau	branch
la rame	oar
le ramage	warbling
le gazouillement	prattle, twitter
l'écume, f.	foam, dross
le puits	well, shaft
le peuplier	poplar
l'orme, m.	elm

le frêne	ash
le hêtre	beech
le mélèze	larch
l'érable, m.	maple
le bouleau	birch
le sapin	fir
le platane	plane-tree
le tilleul	lime-tree
le chêne	oak
le châtaignier	chestnut-tree
le noyer	walnut-tree
le marronnier	chestnut-tree
la chair	flesh
la chaire	pulpit
la chère	cheer, fare
l'aune, m.	alder
l'aune, f.	ell
le sureau	elder
le saule	willow
l'yeuse, f.	holm oak
le cahot	jolt
le caillot	clot
la courroie	leather strap
la sangle	strap
la lanirère	thong
l'enflure, f.	swelling, bombast
la ruelle	lane, bed-side
la meule	mill-stone, grindstone
le beffroi	bell-tower, alarm-bell
l'emplette, f.	purchase
le cachot	black hole, dungeon
le caniche	poodle dog
le lévrier	greyhound [hound
le limier	lime-hound, blood
l'arête, f.	fish-bone, edge
le noyau	stone, nucleus
l'emeute, f.	riot
la meute	pack (of hounds)
l'aubaine, f.	godsend
la charrue	plough
la herse	harrow, portcullis
le pont-levis	draw-bridge
la flèche	arrow, spire
la houlette	crook
le cadeau	present
le carquois	quiver
la gerbe	sheaf

la houle	swell
le givre	rime
la rafale	squall
la bourrasque	squall
la bise	north wind
le grain	grain, squall, shower
la vareuse	guernsey-smock, pilot
la redingote	frock coat [coat
le revers	back, facing, top
	(of boot), reverse
le velours	velvet
la roue	wheel [(honey)
le rayon	ray, spoke, comb
le moyeu	nave
la jante	felly
la giboulée	shower
l'if, m.	yew tree
le houx	holly-tree
l'équipée, f.	trick, prank [party
la corvee	statute-labour, fatigue
le braconnier	poacher
le renfort	reinforcement
la claque	slap, smack, clappers
le soufflet	slap in the face, bellows
l'attente, f.	waiting, expectation
l'atteinte, f.	blow, injury
la tentative	attempt
le pan	skirt, piece
le carrefour	cross-road, public place
la loge	cell, box
la ruche	hive
le roussin	thickset stallion
le grison	donkey
le baudet	jack-ass
la bourrique	she-ass
le porte-faix	porter
l'outre, f.	leathern bottle
l'accueil, m.	reception
la foudre	lightening
le glaive	sword
le tréteau	stage, trestle
le seuil	threshold
le deuil	mourning
le chassis	sash, frame
le mastic	putty, cement
la bourre	flock, wad
la bure	drugget, shaft (mining)
la natte	mat, plait

l'aiguillon, m.	sting, stimulus
le soc	plough-share
le sarrau	smock frock
la bourriche	basket
le sarrasin	buck-wheat
le feu-follet	will o' the wisp
la gaine	sheath
le fourreau	sheath
le scrutin	ballot
la fougue	passion, spirit, mettle
la gamelle	solder's tin
la bandoulière	shoulder-belt
le marais	marsh
le marécage	moor, swamp
le bourbier	slough
le courroux	anger
le grelot	bell
le laiton	brass [sow-thistle
le laiteron	hare's lettuce,
le rateau	rake
la houe	hoe [man
le laboureur	ploughman, husband
la nuance	shade, tint
la nue	cloud
la nuée	cloud, multitude
le rez-de-chaussée	ground-floor
la chaussée	causeway
la chaussure	shoes, boots
la chaussette	sock
la treille	vine-arbour, vine-stalk
le treillis	lattice
la culasse	breech
la crosse	butt-end
le calibre	caliber, bore, size
le canon	barrel, cannon
le haillon	rag
la guenille	tatter, rag
la soie	silk, bristle
le gueux	beggar, scoundrel
la besace	wallet
le faisceau	bundle, pile
la hanche	hip, haunch
la boussole	sea-compass
le chiffre	cipher, figure
l'échantillon, m.	sample
le maraîcher	kitchen-gardener
la butte	rising ground
le but	aim, mark

le bout	end, tip
le croquis	sketch
le cauchemar	night-mare
l'orgueil, m.	pride
la paroi	side, partition-wall
la cloison	partition [splendour
l'éclat, m.	fragment, piece,
l'obus, m.	shell
la récolte	crop
la moisson	harvest
la vendange	vintage
la girouette	vane
le flambeau	torch
le lambeau	shred, piece
la loque	tag, tatter
la défroque	old clothes
la denrée	food, commodity
la disette	dearth
la menotte	handcuff, little hand
le panache	plume
le cimier	crest
la cime	summit
la verve	spirit
la houille	coal
la houillère	coal-pit
le manant	peasant
la luciole	fire-fly
l'ivresse, f.	intoxication
le mûrier	mulberry-tree
la piqûre	prick, sting
le tuteur	guardian
le pupille	ward
la pupille	ward, pupil (of the eye)
la rosée	dew
l'envergure, f.	length of the yards, spread of wings
la passerelle	foot bridge
l'echalier, m.	fence (made of branches of trees)
le pilotis	piling
le poteau	post
le pieu	stake
le plafond	ceiling
le plancher	floor [(of a court)
le parquet	inlaid floor, bar
le lambris	panelling, wainscoting
la serrure	lock
le cadenas	padlock

le piéton	pedestrian
la vigie	look-out man
le fracas	crash
l'epave. f.	wreck, waif
la poutre	beam
la solive	joist
l'enclume, f.	anvil
le poil	hair
le crin	hair
la toile	cloth
l'araignée, f.	spider
l'enfer, m.	hell
le tison	fire-brand
le lien	bond
le timbre	bell, tone, stamp
la toison	fleece
le galet	pebble
le jarret	ham, hock
le coude	elbow, bend
le coudrier	hazel-tree
le faite	top
le comble	heaping, height, zenith
la crèche	crib, manger
la grève	strand, strike
les hardes, f.	clothes
la nippe	clothes
la cheville	ankle
l'aisselle, f.	arm-pit
la laitue	lettuce
la mitraille	grape-shot
le caisson	powder-cart
l'affût, m.	gun-carriage, watch
le fourgon	limbers, wagon [rod
la baguette	switch,drum-stick, ram
la guérite	watch-tower, sentrybox
le piége	snare, trap
le palefrenier	groom
la paillette	spangle
la paillasse	mattress
le paillasse	clown
le faussaire	forger
le cahier	copy-book
la tanière	den
le vivandier	sutler
le cadre	frame, officers
l'enceinte, f.	inclosure
le mépris	contempt

la méprise	mistake
la défiance	distrust
le défi	challenge
l'amende, f.	penalty, fine
la rente	income
le rentier	fund-holder
le badaud	lounger
le flâneur	stroller, lounger
la coulisse	running-string, groove,
le grésil	sleet [side-scene
la vitre	window-glass
la vitrine	shop-window
le carreau	pane of glass, the
	ground [hunger
la fringale	(sudden and excessive)
la fronde	sling
l'écharpe, f.	scarf, sling
le grimoire	scrawl
l'écot, m.	share
le fripier	broker, old clothes-man
le recéleur	receiver of stolen goods
l'entonnoir, m.	funnel
l'esquisse, f.	sketch
l'ébauche, f.	outline
la béquille	crutch
l'avanie, f.	affront
le facteur	postman
la fanfare	flourish of trumpets
le fanfaron	blusterer
l'étape, f.	rations, halting-place
l'étoupe, f.	tow
le penchant	inclination
le fauteuil	arm-chair
le pompon	ornament, tuft
le hangar	shed
le pavillon	pavilion, flag
l'appentis, m.	pent-house
l'égout, m.	fall, sewer
l'évier, m.	sink
le cloaque	sink
l'étrenne, f.	new year's gift
l'arbalète, f.	cross-bow
le pourboire	something for one's self,
	drink-money
le déboire	mortification
l'essieu, m.	axle-tree
le tamis	sieve
le crible	riddle

la cible	target
la simagrée	grimace
le bocage	grove
le bosquet	grove, thicket
l'abattoir, m.	slaughter-house
le camet	note-book
le calepin	scrap-book, memorandum book
la carnassière	game-bag
le charnier	charnel-house
la charnière	hinge
le gond	hinge
le poignet	wrist
la poignée	handful, handle
la jactance	boasting
la banlieue	suburbs
la bêche	spade
la pioche	pick-axe
le poêle	stove
la poêle	frying pan

VERBS.

mouiller	to wet
franchir	to wet to leap over, cross
froisser	to bruise, clash with
frotter	to rub
meurtrir	to bruise
prodiguer	to lavish
arpenter	to survey, measure, walk rapidly
altérer	to make thirsty, alter (for the worse)
asséner	to strike, deal (a blow)
assommer	to fell, beat to death, knock down
bousculer	to hustle
entamer	to cut, begin, broach
soupirer	to sigh
épuiser	to exhaust [accost
aborder	to approach, run foul of,
semer	to sow
récolter	to reap
moissonner	to harvest
vendanger	to gather
glaner	to glean
culbuter	to throw down head over heels, overthrow

reculer	to move back, postpone
acculer	to drive into a corner
roucouler	to coo
chatoyer	to play (of colour)
chatouiller	to tickle
baiser	to kiss
baisser	to lower [dart
darder	to shoot with a dart,
embrasser	to embrace, kiss
embraser	to fire, set on fire
contre-carrer	to thwart, cross
morigéner	to reprimand, lecture
gêner	to inconvenience, impede, hinder
ôter	to remove, to take away
oser	to dare
gonfler	to inflate, swell
crever	to burst, die
éclater	to burst
emmener	to take away
haleter	to pant for breath
s'ébouler	to fall down
s'écrouler	to fall in
s'effondrer	to fall in, give way
couler	to flow, run
s'écouler	to flow away, elapse
se blottir	to cower, squat
sangloter	to sob
grelotter	to shiver with cold
chuchoter	to whisper
attiser	to poke, stir up
arborer	to erect, set up, hoist (a flag)
hisser	to hoist
héler	to hail, challenge
manier	to touch, manage
menager	to husband, spare
octroyer	to grant [seize
s'emparer de	to take possession of,
goûter	to taste
dégoûter	to disgust
dégoûtter	to drop
ronger	to gnaw
rougir	to blush, redden
rugir	to roar
tarir	to dry up
fourvoyer	to mislead

rebrousser	to turn back [down
terrasser	to throw down, knock
se cotiser	to club together
fredonner	to hum
broyer	to pound
fracasser	to shatter
taquiner	to tease
gratter	to scrape, scratch
égratigner	to scratch
griffer	to claw [graze
effleurer	to take off the surface of,
débarquer	to land
embarquer	to ship
s'embarquer	to embark, go on board
retentir	to resound
s'efforcer	to make an effort, endeavour
tâcher	to endeavour, try
tacher	to spoil, stain
être censé	to be reputed
tâter	to feel
tâtonner	to grope
tousser	to cough
cracher	to spit
moucher	to wipe the nose, snuff
éternuer	to sneeze
ronfler	to snore
bourdonner	to hum, buzz
coasser	to croak (frogs)
croasser	to croak
emballer	to pack up
raser	to shave, graze
tailler	to cut, prune [experience
essuyer	to wipe, go through,
se targuer	to boast
narguer	to set at defiance
se douter de	to suspect
se fier à	to trust
se défier de	to distrust
licencier	to disband
hurler	to howl
heurter	to strike, knock
avaler	to swallow
humer	to inhale
frissonner	to shiver
découper	to carve [squander
gaspiller	to throw into disorder,
gâter	to spoil

frétiller	to frisk
faner	to turn (hay), fade
brûler	to burn
épargner	to economize, spare
anéantir	to annihilate, destroy
éblouir	to dazzle
dresser	to erect, train
biaiser	to slant, shuffle
ravauder	to mend
raccommoder	to repair
amonceler	to heap up
entasser	to heap up, pile up
balbutier	to stammer
éprouver	to try
farder	to paint
braquer	to point
tricoter	to knit
nuire	to injure
mirer	to aim
pencher	to incline
surplomber	to overhang
surmener	to overdrive
surfaire	to overcharge
croiser	to cross, cruise
appuyer	to support
exaucer	to hear, grant
exhausser	to raise
étendre	to extend
éteindre	to extinguish
atteindre	to reach
entendre	to hear
attendre	to wait for
attendrir	to make tender, move the feelings
étreindre	to clasp
refléter	to reflect
éreinter	to break the back
regimber	to kick, resist
froncer	to contract, knit
répandre	to pour out, spread, shed
enclouer	to spike (a gun)
chômer	to stand still, be idle
détrousser	to rob, plunder
saupoudrer	to salt, sprinkle
grêler	to hail
guetter	to watch
fendre	to split, cut through
feindre	to feign

fondre	to melt, pounce
fonder	to lay the foundation of, found
moudre	to grind, mill
mouler	to mould
recouvrer	to recover
recouvrir	to cover again, cover up
élaguer	to prune, lop off
fouler	to press, trample on, sprain
empiéter	to encroach
défricher	to clear
déblayer	to clear away
baver	to drivel, slaver
hennir	to neigh
mugir	to low
grogner	to growl [attend
vaquer	to apply one's self,
se récrier	to exclaim, cry out
étancher	to stop, stanch
sombrer	to founder
étioler	to etiolate, to blanch
flétrir	to cause to fade, wither, blast [dejected
s'affaisser	to sink, collapse, be
se chamailler	to scuffle, squabble
émousser	to blunt
aiguiser	to sharpen
affiler	to whet
ruer	to hurl, kick
se ruer	to rush [to quarrel
brouiller	to mingle, jumble, cause
se brouiller	to quarrel
se refaire	to refresh one's self, recruit one's health
étrenner	to handsel
chanceler	to totter
guérir	to cure, heal
gravir	to climb
racier	to scrape
louer	to let, hire praisr
nettoyer	to clean
tamiser	to sift
sourciller	to frown
se pavaner	to strut
trébucher	to stumble [(the eyes
dessiller	to unseal, open
parer	to adorn, ward off, parry

ébranler	to shake
écorcer	to bark, strip
écorcher	to skin, flay
écosser	to husk, shell
planer	to hover [dict
dementir	to belie, deny, contra
harceler	to harass
baîller	to gape, yawn
pavoiser	to dress (ship)
fouiller	to search, ransack

ADJECTIVES AND PAST PARTICIPLES.

bossu	hump-backed
bancal	bandy-legged
borgne	one-eyed
bègue	stammering
boiteux	halt
trapu	stubby, squat
louche	squint, equivocal
aveugle	blind
rabougri	stunted [stunned
étourdi	giddy, thoughless,
engourdi	torpid, benumbed
estropié	lame, crippled
crépu	woolly
ahuri	astounded
abasourdi	dumfounded
acariâtre	cross
entêté	obstinate
transi	chilled
grassouillet	plump
revêche	harsh, crabbed
blême	sallow, wan
blafard	palish, wan
clair-semé	thin-sown, rare
majeur	greater, of age
mineur	minor, under age
aîné	elder
cadet	younger
abrité	shelter
abruti	stupefied, besotted
refrogné	scowling, grim
rechigné	crabbed
ridé	wrinkled, rippled

effaré	scared, bewildered
affairé	busy
camus	flat-nosed
cagneux	crook-kneed
émaillé	enamelled
fuyard	fugitive, fleeing
morne	depressed. gloomy
ivre	intoxicated, drunk
soûl	glutted, drunk
enivré	intoxicated
gris	gray, tipsy
crénelé	embattled
basané	sun-burnt
nuancé	variegated
cru	raw, crude
cuit	cooked [inexhaustible
intarissable	never-failing,
inépuisable	inexhaustible
sain	healthy, wholesome
malsain	unhealthy,unwholesome
propre	clean, own
malpropre	unclean
sale	dirty
laid	ugly
unique	only, sole
immonde	unclean, impure
insouciant	heedless, unconcerned
courroucé	incensed
agencé	arranged, fitted up
acharné	infuriated, desperate
hardi	bold
frayé	traced, beaten (roads)
étroit	narrow
droit	straight, right
tortueux	winding
gauche	awkward, left
grossier	rough, coarse
faible	weak
adroit	dexterous, skilful
maladroit	unskilful, clumsy
joufflu	fat-cheeked
banal	commonplace
empressé	ready, eager, zealous
amer	bitter
saumiâtre	brackish
treillissé	lattice
retroussé	turned up
navré	broken-hearted

goguenard	jeering [delicate
scabreux	rugged, perilous,
guilleret	lively
fin	fine, shrewd, cunning
chétif	wretched
mesquin	mean
piette	poor
moisi	mouldy
pourri	rotten
bigarré	party-coloured
raboteux	rough
coiffé	combed, fitted
chaussé	shod
ganté	gloved
rouillé	rusty
aguerri	inured
hâve	wan
outré	exaggerated, exasperated
repu	fed
rassasié	satiated
menu	small
crevé	burst, dead
badin	playful
lambin	dawdling
inepte	unfit [worse
altéré	thirsty, changed for the
recherché	in request, far-fetched,
	studied
facheux	unpleasant
malencontreux	untoward
rétif	restive
fringant	frisky, mettlesome
rauque	hoarse
rogue	haughty
évanoui	fainted
maussade	sullen, cross [knife
à outrance	beyond measure, to the
broyé	pounded
fracassé	shattered
meurtri	bruised
cramoisi	crimson [easily
ombrageux	shy, that takes umbrage
fripé	rumpled
badigeonné	coloured, white-washed
boursoufflé	swollen, bloated
lâche	slack, cowardly
bizarre	whimsical, strange
épars	dispersed, straggling

éparpillé	scattered
ébahi	amazed
bichonné	curled
attifé	bedizened
emporté	passionate, run away
échevelé	with dishevelled hair
égaré	stray, wild
écarté	remote, lonely
criblé	pierced all over, riddled
raide	stiff
excédé	tired out
fade	insipid
jonché	strewed
fêlé	cracked
foncé	dark
harnaché	harnessed
avarié	damaged
bavard	talkative
hargneux	surly
enclavé	enclosed
pailleté	spangled
diapré	variegated
ameuté	hounded on
diaphane	transparent
chamarré	trimmed with lace, bedizened
tapi	crouched
busque	curved
velu	hairy
glabre	hairless, smooth
sanglant	bloody, underdone, offensive
sanguin	sanguine (rich in blood)
sanguinaire	murderous, blood-thirsty
défiant	distrustful, wary
en friche	unploughed
en jachère	fallow
friand	dainty
engoué	infatuated
enjoué	playful
falsifié	falsified, adulterated
frelaté	sophisticated, adulterated
croupi	stagnant
zébré	striped (like the zebra)
moucheté	spotted
tacheté	speckled
affaissé	sunk down, dejected

écarquillé	wide open
rayé	scratched, striped
reculé	remote
acculé	driven into a corner
barbouillé	smutty, daubed
brouillé	mingled, at variance
enroué	hoarse
lézardé	cracked [patronized
achalandé	having custom, well
embauché	engaged
apprivoisé	tame
hâlé	sun-burnt
saccadé	by jerks, abrupt
svelte	slender
sournois	sly
grêle	slim, shrill
éperdu	distracted
fourbe	cheating, knavish
niais	simple, silly
en sautoir	cross-wise
creux	hollow, deep, sunken
interdit	prohibited, speechless,
gouailleur	jeering [sheepish
myope	short-sighted
narquois	mocking

Mr Taylor's Simple Guide to Speaking and Writing French

Approximate pronunciations are in *italics*.

1. Saying who you are.

'Je m'appelle' means literally 'I call myself' but translates nowadays 'my name is'; it is pronounced like' *ger-map-elle'*
If you want to say what someone else is called, you just change 'je' for 'il'(he), or 'elle'(she), and change the 'm' for an 's' (for someone else!)

Je m'appelle Charles Grandorge Ewing.
Elle s'appelle Maud Erskine Crum Ewing.

2. Saying how old you are.

French people do not say how old they are, but how many years they have! So, 'j'ai' (*'jay'*) means 'I have', 'ans'(*ong*) means years. You just put them together with the appropriate number word in between.

J'ai douze (12) ans = I am twelve years old

If you want to say how old someone else is you just swap 'je 'for
Il or elle and take the 'i' off 'ai', because you are not talking about
'I' any more!

Elle a douze ans = she is twelve years old.

3. Saying what you are like

'I am ' is **'je suis' (*ger-swee*)** and you just add an adjective after this BUT… French people pronounce their adjectives slightly differently if they are talking to a lady or young girl. How?

This is easy. In general, if you can hear the last sound of the adjective being used it means that a lady or young girl is being referred to. When you write your adjective, you often have to add an extra 'e' to the end of the word, (possibly because you are talking about *e*lle!)

Je suis bavard (bav-ar), I am chatty (a boy talking)

Je suis bavarde (*bav-arde*), I am chatty (a girl talking)

The extra 'e' on the end means that you have to say the final 'd': you can hear the last sound of the word clearly so it refers to a lady or girl speaking.

'Elle est' means she is, 'il est' means he is.

Other adjectives end in different letters and so the final sound may be different:
marrant (*mar-ong*), with an extra 'e'.
marrante (mar-ont). Adjectives that end in an 'x' swap the 'x' for 'se' and this is pronounced as if it were a 'z'

Elle est parresseuse (*para-surze*), she is lazy.

4. Connecting things up.

Nobody talks as if they were reciting a
shopping list (although I do know some) at
least, they *should* not ! So you now have to
learn how to join one phrase onto another
using connecting words.

Et (*eh*), and; aussi (*oh-si*), also; puis (*pwee*),
then; mais (*may*), but
These four are essential to get you started!

Je m'appelle Grandorge et j'ai douze ans. Je
suis bavard et marrant. Maud, ma soeur,
elle est marrant mais aussi parresseuse.

What do you think 'ma soeur' means?
Write down how you say your name and
age and add some phrases describing
yourself.

5. Saying what you like: nouns in French

Before we look at how you actually say 'I
like' or 'I love', we need to look at nouns
(persons, places and things) in French.

All French nouns are either masculine or
feminine (these are called genders). Why?
Well, it comes from the time when France
was part of the Roman Empire. Then, if
you wanted to stay on the right side of the
local Roman Governor, you spoke Latin.
Consequently, as the French language
developed after the Romans left, or were
kicked out, this business of masculine and
feminine nouns stayed a feature of
everyday spoken French.

And you need to know whether a noun in French is feminine or masculine, because each gender has different words for 'a' (or 'an') and 'the'.

6. Natural Gender, naturally…
Now, I have to be very careful here. Obviously, words like sister, mother, aunt are all feminine. You would expect them to be because the noun actually refers to someone feminine. This we call natural gender. So, the words for brother, father, uncle are masculine in French. It would make life so easy if there were just another rule, as simple, to explain the gender of all other words in French. But:

THERE IS NO ONE RULE THAT WILL TELL YOU THE GENDER OF ALL NOUNS IN FRENCH.

Except, and this is where I have to be a little circumspect, often (not always) nouns which you might justifiably expect to have a strong feminine link are indeed feminine and likewise for masculine nouns. Of course, these links in the language were established a long time ago, and so nowadays although the word for, say,' kitchen' in French is indeed feminine (la cuisine) it does not do to labour the point.

Some examples of feminine nouns: maison (house), tasse (cup)
jupe (skirt), vaisselle (washing up)
Some examples of masculine nouns: livre (book), chapeau (hat)
veston (jacket), stylo (pen)

Most nouns in French that are based completely on an English word are masculine:

Le foot (football), le basketball , le badminton

7. Using words for 'the' and 'a/an'
Having established what these words for 'the' and 'a/an' are we now need to look at the very simple rule that governs their use.

ALL FRENCH NOUNS MUST HAVE A WORD FOR 'THE' OR 'A/AN' IN FRONT OF THEM'

(… or a word for 'some' or 'to', but we will look at that later!)

So, whereas in English we can say (and do say) 'I like football',
in French they would say the equivalent of 'I like *the* football', meaning the game of football.
We might say, 'in summer, I like salad', in French they would say the equivalent of ' in summer, I like *the* salad '.

The word for 'the' with all feminine nouns in French is

'la' (*lah*)

The word for 'the' with all masculine nouns in French is

'le'(*luh*)

Just as in English, the French make
something plural (more than one) by
adding an 's' on the end. BUT, annoyingly,
they do not pronounce it.

'Tomate' is pronounced exactly as the same
as 'tomate**s**'
'Pomme' (apple) is pronounced exactly the
same as 'pomme**s**'

So, if the final 's' is not pronounced, how
are you going to know whether someone is
talking about one bar of chocolate or ten?
(This could be very important!)

**The answer is that in French, when you
have a noun in the plural, you use a
different word for 'the', which if you like
signals that the very next word is plural.
This word is**

'les' (*leh*)

Use of 'a/an' is much easier: you use these
words just as you would in English :
I like a tomato (une tomate) with my salad
I prefer a coffee (un café) after my dinner

Again, one is feminine, one masculine.

The word for 'a/an' with feminine nouns is

'une' (*ewn*)

**The word for 'a/an' with masculine nouns
is**

'un'(*uh*)

The plural word for these both is

       'des' (*deh*) = some

A word of caution!

Despite what you may think, French is a
very precise language!
It is very rare that you find 'ambiguity'
(more than one meaning possible in a
single phrase).

So, if you say 'I like coconuts' (in French, I
like *the* coconuts) it means you like *all*
coconuts, without exceptions!
You have to be careful when you go
shopping: if you say (in French, of course)
'I want to buy the lettuces' (meaning
'some' lettuces, the poor old French
greengrocer will assume you have decided
to buy *all* his lettuces and not just the few
that you think you are buying!

8. Verbs (doing words) : aspects of love

Using most French verbs really could not
be easier!

First, you must remember that

in French:

'I eat cabbages'

is the same as

'I am eating cabbages'

is the same as

'I do eat cabbages'

(all present tense, describing what is
happening *now*)

THE SAME PHRASE IN FRENCH MEANS
ALL OF THESE AT THE SAME TIME,
WHEN TRANSLATING FRENCH YOU
SIMPLY PICK THE ONE THAT MAKE
MOST SENSE.

The above phrases in English are known as
the different 'aspects'
of the verb. Later on, we will look at the
equivalent phrases of the verb 'to like' (or
'to love'… aspects of love, you could say!)

9. How to use most French verbs (doing words) in the present tense

Part One

First of all, you must remember that in French, if a word, any word, including verbs, finishes with

'er'

then that bit on the end must be pronounced like

'eh'

as if you were saying 'egg', but without the 'gg'.

It is the 'r' on the end which means that this has to be pronounced in this way.

Once you understand this, you are **half way** to using most French verbs completely accurately in the present tense!

> If it is written with 'er' on the end
> it is pronounced   'eh'

Part Two

MOST FRENCH VERBS END IN 'ER', WITH, THEREFORE, AN 'EH' SOUND ON THE END.

Some examples: manger (*monjeh*) = *to* eat
jouer   (*jooeh*)   = *to* play
porter   (*porteh*) = *to wear*

This form of the verb is known as an *infinitive*

You will notice that the **ONE** word in French (manger)is equal to **TWO** words (to eat) in English.

(One way of remembering this is to pretend that the 'r' ('eh') part means the 'to' before the verb in English (it doesn't, but it is a useful way of remembering this rule!)

So, if you take the 'r' ('eh') away from the end of the verb, you are left, of course, with the first sound that remains.

Mange (-r) = *'monj'*
Joue (-r)   = *'joo'*
Port (-r)   = *'port'*

(don't worry, this isn't getting like maths, I promise !)

… AND THAT IS IT! YOU CAN NOW USE MOST FRENCH VERBS IN THE PRESENT TENSE AND I WILL SHOW YOU HOW!

First of all,
I = je *(ger)*, he = il *(eel)*, she = elle *(ell)*, on = we *(ong)*

… and all you have to do is add the French verb, but without the '-r' ('-eh') on the end.

So, I eat/I am eating/I do eat   = je mange (*'ger monje'*)
I play/I am playing/ I do play = je joue (*'ger joo'*)
I wear/I am wearing/I do wear = je porte (*'ger port'*)

And you can replace 'je' with the word for 'he', 'she' or 'we' and the verb stays exactly the same.

This is how most verbs which end in 'er' work.

This little song will help you to remember some of these verbs in French. It works well if sung to the tune of 'Courting in the kitchen' which is a traditional Irish folk song.

J'arrive à neuf heures pile
I arrive at nine o' clock on the dot

Je parle avec mes copains
I talk with my friends

Je mange à la cantine
I eat in the kitchen

J'adore manger du bon pain
I love to eat good bread

À onze heures et demie
At half past eleven

J'écoute le professeur
I listen to the teacher

J'aime beaucoup travailler
I like very much to work

Avec l'ordinateur!
With the computer!

10. Saying what you do not do
To change 'I eat' into 'I do not eat/I am not eating'

You just put 'ne' before the French verb and 'pas' after it.

So, ' je mange' becomes 'je **ne** mange **pas**'
     (I eat)   (I do not eat)
Saying what you do not have

I have = j'ai
I do not have is 'je n'ai pas' (you lose the 'e'
from the 'ne' because there is a vowel
coming after it, and often you cannot have
two vowels together in this way).

BUT: if you are saying what you do not
have, you must, in French, follow 'je n'ai
pas' with 'de', then followed simply with
the word, or words, for the thing or things
that you do not have.

Learn this refrain! Once you learn how to
say that you do not have any chewing gum
(which you should not have anyway) you
can automatically talk about anything else
you do not have.
Je n'ai pas de chewing gum,
I haven't got any chewing gum
Je n'ai pas de chewing gum,
I haven't got any chewing gum
J'ai du café, j'ai du rhum,
I have some coffee, I have some rum
Mais surtout pas de chewing gum
But especially not any chewing gum.

(I have chosen the word for that famous
Jamaican import and erstwhile favourite of
Jolly Jack Tar simply and only because it
happens to rhyme with the word 'gum').

11. Aspects of love!

The verb in French 'to like/love' is an 'er' verb.

$$aimer = to\ like/love$$

and it behaves in exactly the same way as all other 'er' verbs in French!
So, in order to use this verb ' aimer' with je, il, elle or on
all you have to do is take off the final 'r'.

When using 'je', the French take off the last 'e' of 'je'
to make it easier to say.

So, J'aime = I like/I love (or I am liking/loving)
Il aime = he likes/he loves (or he is liking/loving)
Elle aime = she likes/ she loves (or she is liking/loving)
On aime = we like/love (or we are liking/loving)

So you can now:
Say your name, age and what you are like.

Say what other people are called, their age and what they are like.

You can also connect phrases up using et, aussi, puis, mais.

You can also say what you and others like, using correct words for 'the' and 'a' or 'an'.

You can now also say what you like to do.

12. Saying how often you do something

In English we say things like : I often play football,
he is always eating chocolate, she sometimes listens to music.

The word 'often', 'always' and sometimes come after I, he, and she, and before the verb in the sentence.

IN FRENCH, THESE WORDS CAN NEVER GO HERE!

As a general rule, the word for 'often', 'always' and 'sometimes ' must come either at the beginning of the sentence, or at the end, or , after the verb.

So, I often play football = Souvent, je joue au foot, or

Je joue au foot souvent,

or

Je joue souvent au foot.

BUT NEVER …   Je souvent joue au foot.

You might be understood, but it would sound as odd as if someone in English started talking backwards!

Other 'frequency words'
Normalement = normally
D'habitude   = usually
Parfois   = sometimes
Toujours   = always

13. Explaining why you are doing something.

In your Nursery Rhyme book you will no doubt have a line which goes like 'Simple Simon went to market **for** to by some pigs'

Here, in older English, the word 'for' is used to explain why Simple Simon was going to market.

This word is now left out of English, but is still has to be used in French.

The simple rule is to remember that

WHEN

'TO'

IN ENGLISH MEANS

'IN ORDER TO'

IT IS TRANSLATED BY

'POUR'

IN FRENCH.

So, I like to go to the cinema (in order) **to** watch films
= J'aime aller au cinéma **pour** regarder les films.

The verb that comes after 'pour' is in its simplest form, that is to say, an infinitive, which as we have seen so far, for most verbs in French, ends in 'er'.

14. Saying what you do instead of something else.

au lieu de = instead of

Except, in English we say 'instead of + verb + 'ing'
Eg: Instead of swimming I like playing billiards

In French, it is even simpler as you just use the infinitive after 'au lieu de'.

Au lieu de nager j'aime jouer aux billiards
(literally, 'instead of to swim…)

15. Saying what you do before you do something else.

Again in English we say before + verb + ing

In French it is even simpler as you use the infinitive after
'avant de'

Avant de nager je joue aux billiards
(literally, before to swim…)

16. The past tense
If you can remember, as I am sure you can, that most French verbs in their simplest forms end in 'er' and these are called infinitives. The sound on the end is like 'eh'.

Eg: regarder = to watch, jouer = to play, manger = to eat

If you take off the 'r', in every case, and put an 'acute' accent over the remaining 'e'…

regardé   joué

mangé

(watched)   (played)

you change the verb from one that that means to (watch)
to a new word that is the equivalent of putting 'ed' on the end in English.
However, this is not the case with 'mangé' as we do not say
'eated' in English, but 'eaten'.

Can you remember how to say your age from earlier on?
You say how many years you *have*.

I have = J'ai
So all you need do now is put 'j'ai' with an 'er' verb in French which has had the 'r' removed and an acute accent placed over the final remaining 'e' (é), and you can now use the past tense in French to talk about what you have done!

J'ai regardé le film et puis j'ai mangé un sandwich.
= I (have) watched the film and then I (have) eaten a sandwich ('have' is often left out in English, but it can never be in french.)

17. Words for 'my'

As you know, all nouns in French (persons, places, things) are either masculine or feminine.

Le = the masculine 'the' word
La = the feminine 'the' word

The feminine word for 'my' is very similar to 'la':

'ma' (*mah*)

The masculine word for 'my' is different:

'mon' (*mong*)

The 'my' word for all plurals is similar to 'les'

'mes'

So, connecting up what we have so far covered:

Je m'appelle Charles et j'ai seize ans.

Je suis bavard et aussi marrant.

J'ai une soeur mais je n'ai pas de frère.

Ma soeur, elle s'appelle Maud.

Elle a douze ans.

Elle est bavarde mais aussi paresseuse.

J'aime la géographie mais je n'aime pas les maths.

Ma soeur aime le français.

Elle écoute la musique.

Au collège on aime manger la salade.

Ma soeur aime aussi aller au collège pour jouer au foot!

Moi, au lieu de jouer au foot j'aime jouer au rugby.

Mais, avant de jouer au rugby, je mange toujours un grand sandwich avec mes amis.

Le weekend dernier j'ai joué au rugby et aussi j'ai joué au foot.

Parfois, j'aime jouer au hockey aussi.

So, it is really very simple to begin to speak and write in French as long as you observe a few basic rules AND STICK TO THEM. Experiment by writing a few sample phrases not just describing who you are and what you are like, but also saying what you like to do and with whom.

Bonne courage!

Peter Taylor
Juillet, 2008